Easiest Way To Get Rich in Real Estate Without Using Your Own Money

WANT TO INVEST IN REAL ESTATE?

Questions You Must Ask Yourself Before You Buy Another Real Estate-Tips for Beginners

Wan Mohd Hirwani Wan Hussain

REAL ESTATE INVESTMENT

WANT TO INVEST IN REAL ESTATE? – QUESTION YOU MUST ASK BEFORE BUY ANOTHER REAL ESTATE-

TIPS FOR BEGINNERS- EASIEST WAY TO GET RICH IN REAL ESTATE WITHOUT LOSING YOUR OWN MONEY

By

WAN MOHD HIRWANI WAN HUSSAIN

Copyright © 2016

FREE REPORT

Free Download

Top Secret Amazon Rolodex of 18,700 Best Selling PRODUCTS!

Download Now

As a way of saying thanks for your purchase, I'm giving a free report that's exclusive to my book and readers.

Finding a niche for online a very important before you starting online business.

In this FREE REPORT. You will Discover how to Find a Red-Hot "Hungry" market in Amazon under a minute!. You will also learn how to Generate Real Money in less than 24 hour.

Plus you will get access to my Confidential List of Highest Commission from Amazon. You can download the FREE Report by clicking here

Go to this link:

http://best.tipsdebt.com/

Do you struggle with knowing what to do when it comes to building an online business?

Most people struggle, a lot. The truth of the matter is that if you do not pick the right niche, or focus on serving people who are willing to pay you, chances are that you will fail. But this doesn't mean you have to figure it all out right away: when I started my online business, I didn't know what I wanted to focus on.

Here is just a preview of what's included in this exclusive report: a) What to Look for in a Niche, and b) Why It's Important To Explore Those Little Known Niches!

c) Why Evergreen Niches Are So Profitable!

d) Finding Products To Promote For Your Given Niche and How To Use Clickbank and Amazon To Propel Your Profits!

e) Finding Profitable Keywords For Your Given Niche!

And Much, Much More!

You can download the FREE Report by clicking here

Go to this link:

http://niche.usahawanakademik.com/

INTRODUCTION

The information provided in this book is designed to provide helpful information on the subjects discussed. The publisher and author are not responsible for any specific health or allergy needs that may require medical supervision and are not liable for any damages or negative consequences from any treatment, action, application or preparation, to any person reading or following the information in this book. References are provided for informational purposes only and do not constitute endorsement of any websites or other sources. Readers should be aware that the website listed in this book may change.

Copyright© 2016

All rights reserved. No part of this publication may be reproduced, distributed, or transmitted in any form or by any means, including photocopying, recording, or other electronic or mechanical methods, without the prior written permission of the publisher, except in the case of brief quotations embodied in critical reviews and certain other non-commercial uses permitted by copyright law.

While attempts have been made to verify that the information contained in this publication is accurate, neither the author nor the publisher assumes any responsibility for errors, omissions, interpretations or usage of the subject matters herein.

This publication contains the opinions and ideas of its author and is intended for informational purposes only. The author and publisher shall in no event be held liable for any loss or other damages incurred the usage of the publication.

Feel free to email me if you need further discussion about the techniques. You can contact me through email at the end of this eBook.

TABLE OF CONTENTS

Introduction

Table of Contents

Legal Notes

Chapter 1. INTRODUCTION

Chapter 2. REAL ESTATE

Chapter 3. TYPES OF ESTATE

Chapter 4. BASIC ELEMENT OG GOOD REAL ESTATE

Chapter 5:INVESTING STRATEGY

Chapter 6. CONCLUSION

Other Books By (Author)

Legal Notes

The information contained in WANT TO INVEST IN REAL ESTATE? – QUESTION YOU MUST ASK BEFORE BUY ANOTHER REAL ESTATE-TIPS FOR BEGINNERS EASIEST WAY TO GET RICH IN REAL ESTATE WITHOUT LOSING YOUR OWN MONEY, and its several complementary guides, is meant to serve as a comprehensive collection of time-tested and proven strategies that the authors of this eBook have applied to substantially increase their monthly passive income revenue.

Summaries, strategies, tips and tricks are only recommendations by the authors, and reading this eBook does not guarantee that one's results will exactly mirror our own results. The authors of WANT TO INVEST IN REAL ESTATE? – QUESTION YOU MUST ASK BEFORE BUY ANOTHER REAL ESTATE-TIPS FOR BEGINNERS EASIEST WAY TO GET RICH IN REAL ESTATE WITHOUT LOSING YOUR OWN MONEY have made all reasonable efforts to provide current and accurate information for the readers of this eBook.

Whether because of the general evolution of the Internet, or the unforeseen changes in company policy and editorial submission guidelines, what is stated as fact at the time of this writing, may become outdated or simply inapplicable at a later date. Great effort has been exerted to safeguard the accuracy of this writing. Opinions regarding similar website platforms have been formulated as a result of both personal experience, as well as the well documented experiences of others.

No part of this publication shall be reproduced, transmitted or resold in whole or in part in any form, without the prior written consent of the authors. All trademarks and registered trademarks appearing in WANT TO INVEST IN REAL ESTATE? – QUESTION YOU MUST ASK BEFORE BUY ANOTHER REAL ESTATE-TIPS FOR BEGINNERS EASIEST WAY TO GET RICH IN REAL ESTATE WITHOUT LOSING YOUR OWN MONEY are the property of their respective owners.

Chapter 1. INTRODUCTION

INTRODUCTION

The Beginner's Guide to Real Estate Investing, my intent has been to cover all topics that first-time real estate investors need to know.

In this book, you'll gain a profit-generating introduction to the complete range of knowledge you'll need to begin building wealth in real estate.

This book is directed toward those readers who want to sample all investment topics in one easy-to-read volume.

CHAPTER 2. REAL ESTATE

REAL ESTATE

REAL ESTATE is a term that includes property – such as vacant land, residential houses, condominiums, and commercial or industrial buildings – as well as all activities concerned with the ownership and transfer of ownership of properties.

This section however, is concerned with identifying those types of real estate, which can produce income. For the beginning and advanced investor, these types of investments are the safest.

Income producing properties include: rental homes, apartment buildings, condos, mobile home parks, office buildings, shop-ping centers, retail and wholesale buildings, warehouses, industrial parks, hotels, motels, rest homes, and certain kinds of vacant land that can be used for recreation or agriculture. Of the properties listed above, rental homes, apartment buildings and condos offer the least risk and re□uire the least amount of expertise.

Rental Homes – Single-family residential properties are easier to handle than most real estate in-vestments. Depending on how well you choose your locations, your skills and time, they also have a great potential for appreciation.

Chapter 3: TYPES OF ESTATE

TYPES OF REAL ESTATE

Apartment Buildings –

Buy apartments near universities. You'll always have students to fill them up.

Condos –

Condos tend to be more risky than single family homes. However, they have one advantage that makes them worth considering. Condos having the same square footage as single family homes, can often be purchased for less, yet rented for the same amount. Thus, it is possible for them to be good income producers.

Mobile Home Parks –

Mobile home parks were once the sign of low-income housing. But, times are changing and new mobile home parks are offering better living conditions. Keep your eyes open for cheap vacant land. Mobile home parks require only a bit of maintenance. Mow the lawn, plow some snow, maybe do a bit of repaving, collect the rent, and pay property taxes. Once the park is full, there isn't much to do but pick up the monthly checks. Contrast that with apartment buildings were landlords are expected to do continuous maintenance on the paint, the elevators, the plumbing . . . an endless list. Commercial Properties – Commercial properties such as office buildings, shopping centers, retail and wholesale buildings, warehouse and industrial. A fairly large number of Canadians reside in large homes they no longer need.

There is now and will likely remain a large unsold inventory of these types of properties largely located in the suburbs parks require expert management. Try and buy in stable downtown areas. Motels and Hotels

– Although hotels are often out of the league of the average investor, motels have possibilities. However, be prepared to have them take up a good portion of your time. Rest Homes – Properly chose sites for rest homes, or community living centers, along with well set-up management structures, can become very profitable.

Vacant Land –

Raw land near cities and in cities can be utilized and developed in several different ways. The chart on the left shows how this can significantly impact on its value. However, although some kinds of recreational and agricultural land can be purchased and used to produce income, most investors should stay away from straight vacant land. In most cases, raw land cannot generate a cash flow. Mortgage payments will need to be made out of your pocket.

Straight Land –

Straight land is located away from civilization centers and has no immediate development potential. It is the kind of ground that is only good for holding the earth together.

Recreational Land Unless you can build an racetrack, shooting range or skiing hill, most recreational land has little value.

Agricultural Land –

You can tell how much farmers are making from their land investment by the number of farmers who are selling out. But, times are changing and new mobile home parks are offering better living conditions. Keep your eyes open for cheap vacant land. Mobile home parks require only a bit of maintenance.

Mow the lawn, plow some snow, maybe do a bit of repaving, collect the rent, and pay property taxes.

Once the park is full, there isn't much to do but pick up the monthly checks. Contrast that with apartment buildings were land lords are expected to do continuous maintenance on the paint, the elevators, the plumbing . . . an endless list.

Commercial Properties –

Commercial properties such as office buildings, shopping centers, retail and wholesale buildings, warehouse and industrial

Urban & Suburban Land –

This land is more valuable because it is near population centers and because of the various ways is can be developed. With this kind of land the law of supply and demand works to your advantage.

Chapter 4. THE "BASIC ELEMENTS OF GOOD REAL ESTATE"

There are five basic elements needed to make a real estate property a good investment:

1. Good location

2. Growing market

3. Eager seller

4. Good income potential

5. Favorable financing

The following real estate investment strategies are aimed at helping you recognize and capitalize on these five basic elements.

A. Good Location

Find locations in good neighborhoods.

When you buy a piece of property, you are also buying a neighborhood. Take a good look around. Is the neighborhood deteriorating or improving? If you are unfamiliar with the neighborhood, talk to city planning staff, local property management firms, and local real estate agents? Find locations that are close to needed amenities. Apartments and homes need to be close to shopping centers, churches, schools and other services. If you're considering a commercial building, determine if there is adequate traffic flow or proximity to working establishments. Homes should also be close to places of employment, shopping centers and churches. The further they are away, the worse their location. Make a thorough study of the rental market in your area. Learn what is in demand and what is not.

B. Growing Market

Become familiar with you own local real estate by studying properties on the market.

Learn all about your particular city, its growth patterns, its depressed areas, where the direction of growth is likely to extend, and where you would like to live yourself. You can find this information by talking to real estate agents, as well as city or country planning departments.

NOTE

Determine if there is an large community of mature people who may soon be looking to trade in their houses for easier condo lifestyles or perhaps homes in luxury mature communities? Do a thorough study of prices in your city. To know what is a good deal and what is not, you must know what the going prices are i.e., How can you know what wholesale is if you don't know what retail is? Look for changes in population. Populations of certain areas change with the economy. This means that if you buy houses in anticipation of growth you will reap rewards. Likewise, you will be able to get better deals when people are leaving.

C. Look for conversion opportunities.

The key to making money on a conversion is to turn subdivisions or land on the lower scale to land higher up. For example, consider converting apartments into office space or condos and farm land into subdivisions.

A apartment can be converted into an office if it is located in the downtown or central part of the city. Usually classic buildings with stately white balconies, adequate parking and in excellent locations, e.g., directly across from the country courthouse, make good conversions. You can also convert high rise buildings into condos. Profits are created because people will pay more to own a condominium than they will to rent it.

D. Eager Seller

Look for owner's who are desperate to sell.

If you find someone who appears willingly to do anything to get rid of a property, you can be sure to get a good deal. However, approach the situation cautiously.

Sometimes, people anxious to sell have very legitimate reasons and the problems that go with their property can't be solved easily.

Therefore, if you are not careful in analyzing what has made them want to sell, you could end up buying the property and then wanting to get rid of it for the very same reason.

The key to making money on a conversion is to turn subdivisions or land on the lower scale to land higher up. Your objective is to determine the owner's problem and then determine if you can solve it. Look for owners who have personal and financial problems. People who might be willing to sell their house more cheaply include people who are eager to retire, experiencing health problems, recently divorced, or transferred to new work location.

E. Favorable Financing

Leverage your investment with other people's money.

You don't need to have money to make money. You only need to know how to find the money. If you don't have it, somebody else does. This is the essence of leveraging and what makes investing in real estate so exciting (and dangerous).

More specifically, it works this way:

Find bargain income producing properties, with a positive cash flow, and then buy them (or rather get control of them) with little or no money down. For example, find a break-even income producing property with a value of $240,000 at 20% below market rate ($192,000), and purchase it with a 10% down payment ($19,200). Hold the property for one year. If the property increases in value by 7% during this period, and you were able to get its full value when you sold it, you would now have $256,800 – a profit of $64,800. This is equivalent to a whopping return on your investment of $64,800/$19,200 = 338 percent. If you would have put your money in the bank instead and received 10% per year, you would have $22,000. By leveraging your money, you have made it grow more than 3 times.

Try and meet the needs of the seller.

The best and most satisfying negotiation to both parties concerned – you and the seller – are those in which you try to understand the needs of the seller, and then try to structure your offers to meet these needs.

Turn the seller into a partner.

If you have difficulty in finding partners to invest in property, keep in mind that the partner can be the seller himself. One of the ways you can do this is lease an under-rented property from the seller who is eager to meet their monthly mortgage payments, and then sublet it. You can make this deal even more attractive by asking the seller of the property for a lease with an option to buy.

Write up your own mortgage agreement

  – Create a seller's note.

A "seller's note" is a legal contractual agreement written up by you and the seller regarding how a piece of real estate will be paid for.

It is essentially an mortgage carried by the seller. The advantage of this type of mortgage is the increased flexibility it can give you over bank mortgages, regarding when and how payments are made. For example, to help create a positive cash flow property, and thus make it more favorable for purchase, you can try and structure a seller's note in the following three ways:

- Make mortgage payments that take into consideration seasonal demands e.g., pay

more when your utilities are less and less when they are more.
- Structure a balloon mortgage i.e., pay no monthly sums until the end of the year where you pay a lump sum.
- Increase the length of the amortization i.e., make payments for a thirty-year period but have the option of making a lump sum payment after seven years. Have interest payments smaller the first year and larger in the later years.

KNOW THIS!

One powerful financing technique lies in allowing sellers to borrow out 100 percent of their equity in the real estate holdings. For example, if a seller wants their $15,000 in equity out of their investment right away, you can suggest to them that you will take out a $15,000 mortgage on the property. You then pay the monthly mortgage payments to the bank, as well as the monthly pay-ments to the seller less the $15,000.

Chapter 5: Choose Your Real Estate Investing Strategies

Choose Your Real Estate Investing Strategies

The section above looked at a number of different investment vehicles that you can use to invest in real estate. However, when learning how to invest in real estate, it is not enough to simply know what these property niches are. Instead, as an investor you will use a variety of strategies when dealing with these investment niches to produce wealth. The section below explores three of the most common strategies that you can use to make money with these vehicles.

Buy & Hold

Perhaps the most common form of investing, the "buy and hold strategy" involves purchasing a property and renting it out for an extended period of time. It's probably the most simple and purest form of real estate investing that there is.

Essentially, a "buy and hold investor" seeks to create wealth by renting the property out and either collecting monthly cash flow or simply holding the property until it can be sold for a gain in the future.

Among the advantages of this strategy is that during the time that you hold the property and rent it out, the mortgage is paid down each and every month, decreasing your principal balance and increasing your equity in the property.

One of the most important things for a new buyand hold investor to understand is how to evaluate deals and opportunities. By far the most common mistake that we see new investors make with this strategy is buying bad deals because they simply don't understand propertyevaluation. Other common problems include underestimating expenses, making bad decisions on tenant selection, and failing to manage properly.

These mistakes can all be avoided, however, if you simply learn the business; jumping in without proper education can be extremely costly financially and sometimes, legally.

To properly carry out the buy and hold strategy, an investor should learn how to properly identify the ebbs and flows of the market that a property is located in. Ultimately, when they perceive the market and the properties they are interested in to be at a low point (prices low, inventory high), the buy and hold investor seeks to purchase properites. When the market becomes over heated, an experienced buy and hold investor will usually stop buying until they see things settle back down. During these slow periods, they may sell or simply continue to hold their properties. Some buy and hold investors never sell a property, choosing instead to pay the mortgage off and live on the cash flow or may ultimately sell using "Seller Financing".

Flipping Real Estate

One of the most popular tactics for making money in real estate, due largely to the numerous shows on cable TV that promote it, is flipping houses. House flipping is the practice of buying a piece of real estate at a discounted price, improving it in some way, and then selling it for a financial gain. In reality, the flipping model is quite similar to the "buy low, sell high" model of most retail businesses.

The most popular type of property to flip is the single family home. Following a rule of thumb known as the 70% rule, an experienced house flipper will buy a home for 70% of its current value less any rehab costs. For example: Home A should be worth $100,000 if it were in good condition, but it needs $20,000 worth of work.

A typical house flipper will purchase the home for $50,000 ($100,000 x70%-$20,000) and seek to sell it for the full $100,000 when completed. This is simply a rule of thumb, and actual numbers must be verified and adjusted to ensure a successful and profitable flip.

One of the key aspects in flipping a house is speed. A house flipper will attempt to buy, rehab and sell the property as quickly as possible to ensure maximum profitability and to avoid many months of expensive carrying costs. These carrying costs include monthly bills such as financing charges, property taxes, condo fees (if applicable), utilities and any other maintenance bills required to keep the house in good financial standing.

Flipping is not a "passive" activity, but instead is just like an active day job. When an investor stops flipping, they stop making money until they begin flipping again. Many investors choose to use flipping to fund their day-to -day bills, as well as provide financial support for other, more passive investments.

Wholesaling Real Estate

Wholesaling is the process of finding great real estate deals, writing a contract to acquire the deal, and then selling the contract to another buyer. Generally, a wholesaler never actually owns the piece of property they are selling; instead, a wholesaler simply finds great deals using a variety of marketing strategies, puts them under contract, and sells that contract to another for an "assignment fee." This fee is typically between $500 and $5,000 on average or more depending on the size of the deal. Essentially, the wholesaler is a middleman who is paid for finding deals.

Some wholesalers sell their contracts to retail buyers, but most sell their contracts to other investors (often house flippers) who

Are typically "cash buyers." When dealing with these cash buyers, a Wholesaler can often get paid within days or weeks and can build solid connections in the real estate community.

Many investors choose to begin with wholesaling due to its reputation of being an easy strategy and one with low startup costs when first beginning. Because the property is never actually owned by the wholesaler,

There are no rehab costs, loan fees, contractors, tenants, banks, or other complications. Wholesaling is the most popular strategy taught by real estate gurus and often receives the most attention as a result, though it

Is not as easy to become a successful wholesaler as they make it sound.

Wholesalers must continually seek out the best deals in order to have inventory to sell to others and must have a well designed marketing funnel to continually attract these leads. Wholesalers also must continually seek out buyers for the deals they ac□uire. While promoted as a strategy that anyone can do --even someone with ZERO money --you ultimately do need to have financial resources to build your marketing funnel. That said, those who persist in growing their wholesaling skills often find great success and a good source of income while they grow their knowledge of other, more profitable strategies.

BUILD YOUR TEAM

While as an investor you are required to wear many different hats, you don't need to (and can't) wear all of them. Instead, you need a team. When we refer to "team," we're not suggesting you go out and hire a team of employees to work under you. A "team" is merely a collection of individuals in various different businesses that you can rely on help you move your business forward. Here's a brief look at who should be on any winning.

Real estate investing team:

Your Mentor- Every successful entrepreneur needs a good mentor: a guide. By training under the watchful eye of one smarter than us, we can only get smarter. For more information on mentors. Mortgage Broker/Loan Officer-A mortgage broker is the person responsible for getting you loans especially if you are going "conventional" (not hard or private money). You want someone who has the experience of working with other investors, and you want that person to be creative and smart. Many loan officers have a pipeline of buyers (or future buyers); real estate investors can use the help of local loan officers to build a list of buyers and lease purchasers for their properties.

Real Estate Attorney

-It is important to have someone on the team who can go through contracts and who knows the legalities of all your moves. Don't try to pinch pennies by ignoring this valuable member of your team. You don't need to meet for hours with your attorney each week, but want someone to be available when you need them. Having an attorney who is skilled with real estate investing is highly important for the success of your career. Keep in mind, attorneys can also be compensated through fees collected at acquisition or disposition of a property.

Escrow Officer or Title Rep

-If you live in a state that uses Title & Escrow companies, your escrow officer or title rep is the person responsible for closing a deal. a good one on the team helps to close deals that much quicker. You always want people looking out for YOUR interests.

Accountant

-As you acquire properties, doing your own taxes and bookkeeping becomes increasingly difficult. As soon as possible, hire an accountant (preferably a Certified Public Accountant). Your numbers guy should also be well aware of the ins and outs of real estate and preferably own rental properties of their own. Come tax time, this is the man to help you through the write offs. A good tax accountant will save you more than they cost.

Insurance Agent

-Insurance is a must, and as an investor, you will probably be dealing with a lot of insurance policies. Be sure to shop around for both the best rates and the best service. Do not skimp out on getting insurance, as you never know when you'll need that policy.

Contractor

-A good contractor seems like the hardest team member to find, but can often make or break your profit margin. You want someone who gets things done on time and under budget! Be sure that your contractor is licensed/bonded/insured to protect you. Don't simply hire the cheap guy.

Supportive Family & Friends

-Having the support and backing of loved ones is important in any endeavor. If your spouse or family is not on board, don't invest until they are.

Realtor

-An exceptional real estate agent is fundamental in your investing career. You or your spouse may even choose to become a real estate agent yourself to gain access to the incredible tools that agents have.

Either way, having a agent who is punctual, a go getter, and eager, is important. Real estate agents are paid from the commission when a property is sold. In other words for the buyer, an agent is FREE. They can be an excellent resource for contract real estate work, which may include the following activities: bird dogging, referring buyers, showing properties, open houses, broker price opinions, etc.

Property Manager

-If you don't want to actively manage your properties, a good property manager is important to have.

A good property manager can be hard to find but finding one who can efficiently manage your rentals will make your life significantly easier.

Great Handyman

-Someone to take care of the little things that come up on a daily basis is imperative to have on board. Ask for referrals from other landlords for the best handymen; they typically don't need to advertise, but work almost entirely on referrals from a small group of investors and homeowners.

One of the best sources for finding these team members is through referrals from other investors. In general, another investor would be happy to refer their handyman, mortgage broker, or accountant to you because it reflects well on themselves and their relationship with that professional. Try asking around at your local real estate investor club or here on Bigger Pockets, and you'll be well on your way towards putting the pieces in place

Chapter 6: <u>CONCLUSION</u>

A great real estate team is defined by their ability to consistently produce reliable RESULTS. As you might suspect, that's WAY more difficult to construct in real life than it is to talk about it.

Investors, especially ones with either large portfolios or those who flip a lot (often both), rely on their team daily. When one member fails, the entire endeavor suffers, sometimes to the point of sabotaging the team's goals altogether. Whether you're serving clients, flipping properties, or keeping track of your rentals, your team must consistently produce and avoid the "Excuse Train" at all costs. There are those who do and those who make excuses. The latter will pull you down faster than you can imagine.

Where to Find Real Estate Investments

When you have your criteria set, it's time to start looking for your investment property. No doubt you've seen "For Sale" signs in front of homes, but there are many other ways to find investment properties. This section will explore various ways that you can use to find properties, the list is not exhaustive, but a good start for any new invest investor.

The MLS

The MLS, short for the multiple listing service, is a collection of properties for sale by different real estate brokers across the country.

The Newspaper

While quickly fading from use, the classified section of your local newspaper is a good place to look for homes that are for sale by owner. Oftentimes, real estate agents will also put their listing in the newspaper, so it can be a bit challenging to determine what is listed on the MLS and what is not.

Word of Mouth

Some homes are simply sold the old fashion way by word of mouth. By letting everyone one know that you in the market to buy (and defining your criteria, as discussed above), you place yourself in the best position to find deals via word of mouth. You can also use craiglist and out of bound market.

ABOUT THE AUTHOR

Dr Wan Mohd Hirwani Wan Hussain
wmhwh@ukm.edu.my

I am an enthusiastic and professional, who enjoys being part of, as well as leading, a successful and productive team. I am quick to grasp new ideas and concepts, and to develop innovative and creative solutions to problems. I am able to work well on my own initiative and can demonstrate the high levels of motivation required to meet the tightest of deadlines. Even under significant pressure, I possess a strong ability to perform effectively.

Dr Wan Mohd Hirwani Wan Hussain Ph.D is a university researcher at Graduate School of Business, UKM and internet marketing entrepreneur. He has been involved in internet marketing since 2006 and have many product in varies in e-book and mobile application. He has published numerous articles in international conference and journal publication. Specialties: Internet Marketing, Search Marketing, eCommerce, Search Engine Optimization, SEO, Search Engine Marketing, SEM, Mobile Marketing, Sponsored Advertising.

Having over 8 years' experience in internet marketing, search engine marketing (SEM), search engine optimization (SEO), business development, product, service and internet marketing, he knows how to cost-effectively bring products and services to the internet market place. He has consulted with hundreds of customers about their business, ecommerce and internet solutions, helping them ensure a return on their technology investment.

Google analytics, Google adwords, Facebook advertising, Twitter, Pinterest, Linkedin, Google+.

OTHER BOOKS BY (AUTHOR)

Please check my other e-book.

	http://www.amazon.com/DISCOVER-ULTIMATE-MAKING-ONLINE-INTERNET-ebook/dp/B00K0LBHS8/ref=sr_1_2?s=digital-text&ie=UTF8&qid=1435036865&sr=1-2&keywords=100+per+day
	http://www.amazon.com/Student-Entrepreneurship-Innovation--Business-Strategy-ebook/dp/B00TESIQK0/ref=sr_1_3?s=digital-text&ie=UTF8&qid=1435036974&sr=1-3&keywords=student+entrepreneurship

	http://www.amazon.com/REVEAL-WRITING-ARTICLES-TOPICS--ONLINE-ebook/dp/B0107NFHY8/ref=asap_bc?ie=UTF8
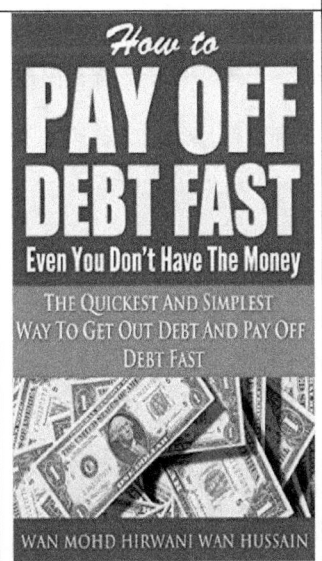	http://www.amazon.com/DEBT-FAST--MONEY--QUICKEST-SIMPLEST-ebook/dp/B013FJE6PM/ref=asap_bc?ie=UTF8

	http://www.amazon.com/INVESTING-INVEST-CREATE-WEALTH-RETIREMENT-ebook/dp/B01A0UEBBI
	http://www.amazon.com/gp/product/B01C8EP3BQ?*Version*=1&*entries*=0

HOW TO MAKE MONEY FROM BLOGS IN YOUR SPARE TIME **CAN YOU MAKE MONEY FROM BLOGGING?** PROVEN AND TESTED TIPS ON MAKE MONEY FROM BLOGS AND BUILD YOUR OWN INTERNET EMPIRE- SIMPLE GUIDELINES Wan Mohd Hirwani Wan Hussain	http://www.amazon.com/gp/product/B01COSN2E6?*Version*=1&*entries*=0
Easiest Way To Get Rich in Real Estate Without Using Your Own Money **WANT TO INVEST IN REAL ESTATE?** Questions You Must Ask Yourself Before You Buy Another Real Estate-Tips for Beginners Wan Mohd Hirwani Wan Hussain	http://www.amazon.com/gp/product/B01COT39AM?*Version*=1&*entries*=0

	http://www.amazon.com/DISCOVER-ULTIMATE-MAKING-ONLINE-INTERNET-ebook/dp/B00K0LBHS8/ref=sr_1_2?s=digital-text&ie=UTF8&qid=1435036865&sr=1-2&keywords=100+per+day
 	http://www.amazon.com/Student-Entrepreneurship-Innovation--Business-Strategy-ebook/dp/B00TESIQK0/ref=sr_1_3?s=digital-text&ie=UTF8&qid=1435036974&sr=1-3&keywords=student+entrepreneurship

	http://www.amazon.com/REVEAL-WRITING-ARTICLES-TOPICS--ONLINE-ebook/dp/B0107NFHY8/ref=asap_bc?ie=UTF8
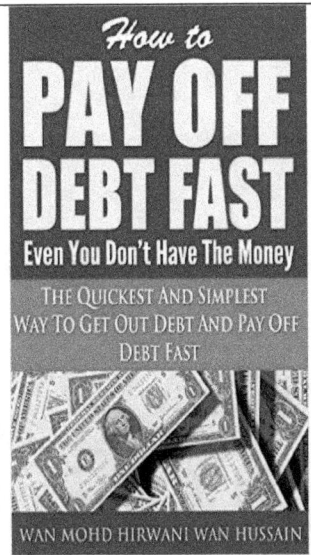	http://www.amazon.com/DEBT-FAST--MONEY--QUICKEST-SIMPLEST-ebook/dp/B013FJE6PM/ref=asap_bc?ie=UTF8

EASY WAYS ON HOW TO INVEST YOUR MONEY, CREATE YOUR WEALTH FOR RETIREMENT — 15 GUARANTEED INVESTING TIPS YOU WISH KNEW — WAN MOHD HIRWANI WAN HUSSAIN	http://www.amazon.com/INVESTING-INVEST-CREATE-WEALTH-RETIREMENT-ebook/dp/B01A0UEBBI
 BEST BUY — INTERNET AND BUSINESS ONLINE — ULTIMATE TIPS TO LEARN HOW TO MAKE MONEY WITH AFFILIATE MARKETING — THE BEST QUICK AND EASY WAYS ON HOW TO START MAKING MONEY ONLINE WITHOUT WEBSITE- MAKE $1000 PER WEEK — WAN MOHD HIRWANI WAN HUSSAIN	http://www.amazon.com/gp/product/B01C8EP3BQ?*Version*=1&*entries*=0

HOW TO MAKE MONEY FROM BLOGS IN YOUR SPARE TIME

CAN YOU MAKE MONEY FROM BLOGGING?

PROVEN AND TESTED TIPS ON MAKE MONEY FROM BLOGS AND BUILD YOUR OWN INTERNET EMPIRE- SIMPLE GUIDELINES

Wan Mohd Hirwani Wan Hussain

FREE REPORT

Free Download
Top Secret Amazon Rolodex of 18,700 Best Selling PRODUCTS!

Download Now

In this **FREE REPORT**. You will Discover

- Find a Red-Hot "**Hungry**" market in Amazon under a minute!
- Generate Real Money in less than **24 hour**.
- My Confidential List of Highest Commission From Amazon.
- Plus, Much, Much More…

Go to this link:
http://best.tipsdebt.com/

Do you struggle with knowing what to do when it comes to building an online business?

Most people struggle, a lot. The truth of the matter is that if you do not pick the right niche, or focus on serving people who are willing to pay you, chances are that you will fail. But this doesn't mean you have to figure it all out right away: when I started my online business, I didn't know what I wanted to focus on.

Here is just a preview of what's included in this exclusive report: a) What to Look for in a Niche, and b) Why It's Important To Explore Those Little Known Niches!

c) Why Evergreen Niches Are So Profitable!

d) Finding Products To Promote For Your Given Niche and How To Use Clickbank and Amazon To Propel Your Profits!

e) Finding Profitable Keywords For Your Given Niche!

And Much, Much More!

You can download the FREE Report by clicking here

Go to this link:

http://niche.usahawanakademik.com/

www.ingramcontent.com/pod-product-compliance
Lightning Source LLC
Chambersburg PA
CBHW070412190526
45169CB00003B/1230